Grá *Mór*

Big Love

Lauren Jade Barton

ISBN: 978-1-914288-30-2

All illustrations and front cover (bar the ones below) by Lauren Barton
Illustrations on page 16 + 29 by Aisling barton
page 54 by Lucy House,
page 64, 69 -74, 76 by Mollie Jean Barton
page 158 by Malana Barton
page 206 by Iona Barton

Dedicated to my soul sister Mollie Jean Barton
without whom these writings would not exist

Downloads...

Contents

as you imagine so shall you be
for to be, you must first imagine

my dreams and imagination save me
over and over again

don't hide your intelligence
the world needs it

Muddy Waters

i do not wish upon you my dark days
but i wish you the grace that my dark days showed me

i sometimes do not feel at all at home in this world
i wonder if other people feel the same

Torn

it can be tough living a physical life when you're more soul
than body

stuck between worlds
a blessing and a curse

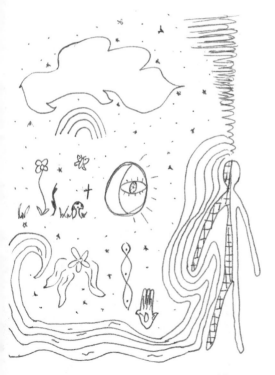

Time Traveller

i sometimes slip into other worlds
and feel a great sense of peace
as if i belong there just as much as i do here
if i am meant to stay here a little while longer
why is it so hard too?

    wandering mind

other worlds call me home
other worlds beyond my own

though tired soul her lifeline thins
the fight to stay here always wins

        heavy figures on the other side

somber days
to match the maze
of thoughts that haze
my weary mind

lonely on a Sunday

~Drawing by Aisling Barton~

unsure which way to grow

painfully aware of my weaknesses…

no one frustrates me more than myself

when i don't measure up to my own expectations

nothing frustrates me more than when i fall short to my own insecurities

so often i stay silent
and say nothing
out of fear of saying the wrong thing
i never want to offend anyone
or for my words to be misconstrued
most of the time what i say doesn't truly reflect
how i feel on the inside
so often talking can be a torment for me
words feel futile
ironically

i must learn the art of speech.

a little scruffy round the edges

-   yours truly.

<u>Adrenaline.</u>

best friend   worst enemy

Anxiety

let it pass
this is not me

a vessel of love's what i am
wait and see

Panic Attack

a surge of energy i can't
contain
coming undone
as i go insane
hold it together you
stupid brain
shame shame
shame shame

jumbled
backwards
the shake in my head
control your thoughts
isn't that what you said?

fumbled all jumbled
my body's a lie
think happy thoughts
let them lift you high
countdown from 10
look yourself in the eye
fear disappear
goodbye
sigh

regain
recover
breathe
you're back
stupid
ugly panic attack

Hesitation

hesitation has been the cause of so many regrets in my life
i've hesitated too long on little decisions
big decisions
people, places and things
like a computer bug that crawls into my system
i momentarily freeze

i forget who i am
what i stand for
and what guides my core

i disassociate to avoid decisions
hoping it'll come to me eventually
but still i wait
i watch thoughts float by in my head
not able to connect to any of them
nervous system unresponsive yet
highly alert in frozen panic
as if to protect me

funny how the outcome is the exact opposite
have i not evolved far from the wild?
have i not caught up with the world
and confronted my inner child?
my soul stuck in a primal past life?

maybe

in need of repair.

Poke

spent my whole day in a maladaptive daydream
huh, funny how you gotta go put a label on that too now
branded like another
has everything gotta be some sort of 'illness' these days?
to make things easier to distinguish for you?
another trait of the human condition
putting labels on sorts only chips away at one's identity
and confidence
makes you feel like there's something wrong with you
how about you just leave it and let it be
can't you see how you're damaging me and the goddamn
rest of society?!

Sliding scales - mood swings

negative default

for God's sake open your eyes

Flip the script already.

a wave of confidence is deceiving
it's only a matter of time before i fuck it all up
before the devil chokes my throat
if they come any closer they'll see the real me
riddled with insecurity
best to retreat to your cave
it's safer there
there there
doubt and low self esteem, we're your friends remember?
we get you
we've got your back
confidence was only trying to trick you
don't listen to her
it's a dangerous world out there

Imposter Syndrome...

Fuck you

We're done.

Her. She. Sis.

18.10.1994

29.04.2015

xxx

no privacy

they watched me on my knees
as you fled from me
cries that shook our ancestors awake

i howled to the moon

we lost you because the answers were not yet out there
i think that's what i was most sorry for
my ignorance

The Aching Heart

pain
heart break
torn
shattered
scream
heart ripped
can't speak
can't breathe
to my knees
i

fall

have you ever held a grown man and woman
your own mother and father
on their knees
bereft by the death of their own daughter?

excruciating
unfathomable
agonising
profound
pain

suddenly you're gone
letting go seems so wrong
i miss you
suddenly you're gone
i'm supposed to be strong
but how do i carry on?
when i miss you

i ache for your presence
from the depths of my core
but time has won
rest in peace
embalmed in love
you now soar

Naive Beginnings

like what even is death?
my brain couldn't fathom it
how can someone be alive one second and then dead the
next?
what stops?
what does that even mean?
what is that?
that force that controls us all?...

that's what i couldn't get my head around
that's what fuelled the burning desire to seek and find out

what makes a heart stop pumping?
what makes muscles stop contracting?

what is that force?

i had to know...

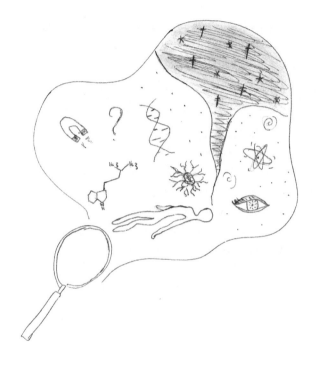

burning curiosity...

Grief is the price you pay for the loss of those you love

but this loss is too heavy on my heart
i cannot fathom how my heart can carry all this pain
and still beat
laboured pulse
poor rhythm
yet still alive
        bitter sweet

to love again, how could i?
if grief is the reward
how does one go on living without mimicking a fraud?
no one informs you of the pain
or how you ever cut the cord
is this the part i beg of you to save me

O holy lord?

Touched by Heaven

i wish i could show you somehow where i went
it was the most beautiful realm i ever did see
i hope to give you glimmers of heaven in all that i do
but to think it's only me who experienced it
my imagination alone
doesn't seem fair
i wish to share that heavenly bliss with everyone
surely it's how God intended the world to be?
surely i'm meant to help others see?
i think i do this through sharing the love inside me
so i must
so i will
share with thee

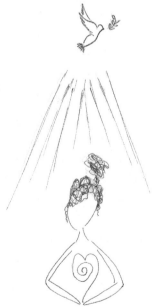

The First Veil
Pt 1

hair floating in dark space
smile so pure and sweet
mischievous, just you
the cutest most angelic face
wee button nose
'Come with me, i'll show you what it was like!'
you spoke
pure joy exhilarated across your face,
like you couldn't wait to take me with you
'tis I
my spirit, in your body
re enacting your final breaths
i remember so clearly, still feel it so viscerally
your body moving my soul, mimicking you
in your final moments
i hear myself from your point of view
singing to you in your right ear
'lavender blue, dilly dilly, lavenders green'
turning to faint whispers as i rise up
my breaths turn from deep to shallow
short sweet breaths as i, once you, gulp for air
sweet baby noises
the purest most heart warming angelic sounds
bitter sweet.
As the breath escapes my lungs,
i gaze into your eyes as you comfort me toward you,
peace and love radiating from your face,
pulling me in
your last breath i take…
weightless
nothing, but everything in one moment
yet not confined by a moment
silence
suspended
stillness…

you lure me in
so close
almost one with you
suddenly, abruptly
i…
'no i can't, i'm not ready!'
but i wanted to go with you so
i was so close to you
next came the swirling vortex, spiralling back down
ricochet through tunnels of bright forceful lights
sucking me back, vibrations so dense
tension
i feel everything
chest thud. thud. thud.
I wake to real time, i'm matter again
breathing frantically backing up into the bed frame
a pool of sweat
dripping
my dear friend beside me, ironically named Molly
shaking me awake
'Lauren are you ok?! you're breathing strange are you ok!?'
blink eyes
breathe deeper
calm, calm, calmmm
shake myself back
what just happened?
frozen, compose
come back
what just happened?

my first veil of you
was it true?

it was you.

45

i cling onto every fragment i have
as i force myself back to sleep
knowing i must wake again soon
scared ill forget every detail
but of course, you have gone before me
how could i ever forgot
you won't let me.

I dance between, awe, and shock
overwhelmed with joy that i was with you
once more
unable to make sense of it
surely it could not be?
but i saw you so vividly.

Days blurred with visions from that night
you came to comfort me, of that i'm sure
i told others in an effort to comfort them
some thought me mad
others i sensed jealousy you did not visit them
'Bless you, it's just a dream'
more passively patronise
but see, you were so happy sis
how could it be?
when your body was hung to the cross
i did see.

Still in the depths of my despair
your message yet untold
i could not fathom
so to return with more you do

so much more…

my biggest blessing just from you…

Pt 2.

the return of you...

Heaven In My Head ...
Sung.
'i saw you last night
heaven in my head
realms of love's where you take me
floating from my bed
pure innocent love, laughter
am i
am i really here, in happy ever after?

angel of my heart
never be apart
angel of my heart
you left me with your mark

i marvelled at you
radiating light
consuming me with your love
all throughout the night
another slip through the veil
so blessed to see
these visits from you
they enlighten me

angel of my heart
never be apart
angel of my heart
you left me with your mark

my angel stay
show me the way
my angel Stay
another day...

'lavender blue'
'lavender's green'
words whispered to you
in reality

rose from your world into tranquility
mmm that harmony it resounds
echoes so graciously
gone before me
to places unseen
truth do i speak
of where you took me
where i've been?
pure innocent love, laughter
was i
was i really there in happy ever after?

my angel stay
show me the way
my angel stay
another day.'

Peace

to die
is just to wake up again
in another moment
to walk through another door
only to arrive in a different time zone
light years away
more blessed than ever before

Parallels

she died for our sin
she died to teach us
she died to forge a new world inside of us
she died to heal us

my guardian angel directed me towards a new sanctuary
a new way of life

Mercy

~Hands drawn by Lucy House ~

My Sister's Love

transcend into your love
Mollie's love
my sister's love
i'm grateful for your gift to me
now i see
enlightened by your love
Mollie's love
your gracious love
opened a door for me
gave me the key
now i see
what you have done for me
showed me what we can be
when souls break free
embody me
Miss Mollie B

with the power of your love

saved by the power of your love

build me a staircase up to your cloud ...

Fly So High

soaring the skies
reaching the light
heaven's arrived

gone are the days of your embrace
wishing i could only see your face
one more time

make no mistake
i've been dreaming awake
one more time

fly so high
soar through the sky
reaching the light
heaven's arrived

breathe in the sight
my soul takes flight
guide me to your light

and so goes the world
and so goes the world

now i'm dreaming awake.

ok i get it
you're everywhere

see i know that you're with me
cause i feel your energy
this might sound kinda crazy
but i know that you've got me

'da da dayyy'
curiosity
won't seem to leave me be

if you know me, you know her

for she lives in here
and i live from here

The Passing Gift

when i can't find the why ...

consult my angel in the sky

Angels
living for two
no, i'm not pregnant

go figure.

eternal bliss from heaven's kiss

heaven's kiss…

eternal bliss

Angel Hugs

i'd get a lot more done if sleep stopped pulling me under

but it's there i see you

our favourite meeting spot

Greyish Blue

i've accepted the grey may always linger
i've made peace with the deep blue
i have disciplined myself not to swim in my emotions
that way
i still function and breathe in the new
that way
i'll continue to see this life through

contentment does come
when you honour
the blue

I refuse to sink

~Drawing by Mollie Jean Barton~

A message to the broken

it's incredibly brave to choose life after a death
incredibly brave
it's even braver to choose life and love
i see you
i'm proud of you
each and every one of you

The phoenix within

you can't escape the fact
that we are
and always will be energy

in some way or another
we are always gonna be energy

never still
never dead

changing colliding
merging fusing exploding
evolving into different forms, shapes and sizes
yes...

but always energy

i hope this realisation brings you as much comfort
as it did me

GRIEF

if you don't face it
it'll face you

PTSD

if you don't face it
it'll face you

ANXIETY, DEPRESSION

if you don't face it
it'll face you

STOP. BREATHE. HEAL.

one day i'll be the one in charge
to see this family through
3 musketeers lost one so dear
and now there's only two
i'll rise to my responsibilities
i'll take it in my stride
for i know that come what may one day
you'll be right by our side

never stop working on me sis
my angel
guide my heart
i promise i'll listen

cause at the end of the day...

'we're all just tryna walk each other home' - Ram Dass

~Drawing by Mollie Jean Barton~

I choose to be diffrent

Be forever young

Ohana

LOL!

Love you lots!

mollie

xxxxx
xxx
xxx
xx
x

~Artwork by
Mollie Jean
Barton

~Artwork by Mollie Jean Barton~

Lyrical   Music

Todays the day i rise above
Hsorrows and pain
From day to day agreed
an endless aching need
for People have lied people haul
cheated bad music is the one way
and that I decide to beat it
ive let them in there let me down.
Ive picked them up have pulled
now undergow to many snakes not
enough ladies. But froba me fron
how on is love that ~~my~~
matters.

its the little things I now # ~~has to~~ tt
bo Facbook # snapchat tt instergrase
you hid behinde em all one
So did ~~g~~ ~~tumbeeta~~ So wassit
~~don fir~~ we had was it really
Just a lie
unwrap yourself dont hid
away for fane to long a high
prial ive had to pay

~ Written by Mollie Jean Barton ~

Chorus

got to Stop running +s
gotta Slow down +3
gotta be brave and
and turn this one around

You Said you cared
You Said you'd be there
but all along you were
the one who Said you
were Scared
you cana run but you
can not hide
the truth one day
will Soon arrive

gotta Stop running+3
gotta Slow down +3
gotta be brave and turn
this one around +s
I wa a foul to fall for your lie
but get this wrong
with

~Written by Mollie Jean Barton~

73

but how through the clouds
i see heres blue skeys.
I'm hungry for the truth
its calling me its what
really moulds its what makes
me me

gets Charout)

~ Written by Mollie Jean Barton ~

knowing your energy lives on forever in all our hearts

fills me with the deepest sense of inner contentment
and peace

Sis,

you have been and will always be my greatest teacher

'for God commands the Angels
to guide you in all your ways'

- Psalm 91;11

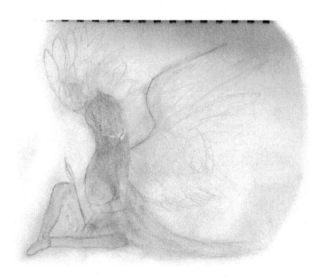

~Drawing by Mollie Jean Barton~

Innsaei

To See From Within

Astral.

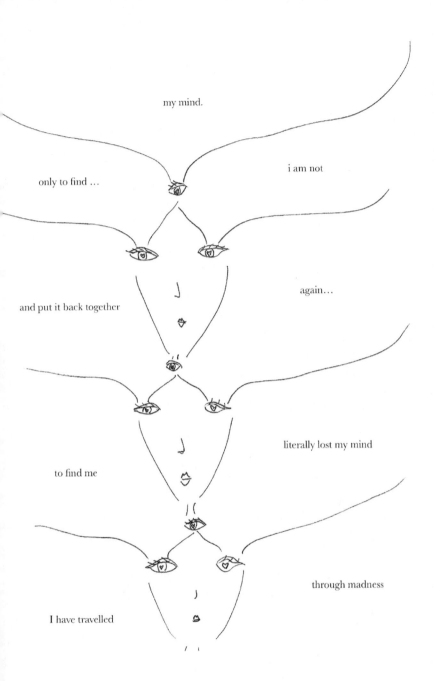

my mind.

only to find ...

i am not

again...

and put it back together

literally lost my mind

to find me

through madness

I have travelled

Astral trip.
Coming undone

slip away
unravel yourself
exposure
slowly slipping

cockroaches
you heightened all my senses
oblivion and beyond
i'm here now

the well within
sucked in
no half measures
do your worst - just like you do your best
red gold glow
plastic monkey

neon sign
old psychic parlour
- Roger Room- LA
cliff top LA

bruce's eyes
my mother's voice
irish mamma

in my dreams - what we made and where we went
into the future back to the past and back 'round again over
and over

multi dimensional perception
lauren AND..... her...

she
my identity was hers

thoughts not words
feeling is language
power of the past
past destruction
words aren't the only way
more than words

violet lights
indigo child
obscure, time displacement
plane coming back
many lifetimes lived in my dreams,
but only minutes in reality
time was no concept
little blue pill
hibernation

rebirth 1
ego death ego kill?
kill ego
ego still.

9 lives linger
surrender

monkey
brain, distraction chew gum
morph to metal, split, airport scanner
wheelchair

1st pulse heartbeat, little finger
reborn again.
the beauty of entering a new life
a vision, entering an embryo
felt first heart beat through little finger
a new home in a mother's womb for now

i'll make peace with my new habitat
i hear doctors voices
inside your womb
shoulder first through the tunnel of life to earth i go

your absence doesn't feel right
sunken back — sink   depression heart drop
distortion
firm grip
i know nothing
slate wiped clean
eternally free
through me -
things don't happen to us they happen through us, pass
through us, but not without affecting every cell in our body
example - an atom a single cell
collateral effect.
Damaged or beautiful
good or bad
just vessels

my imagination saved me
crossing borders - reincarnation
monk preserved in a glass case
monk wink
morph into another life
rebirth
metamorphosis
memories still linger forever etched in my DNA
DNA reconstruction
Rewrite my DNA
DNA healed.

DNA

the invisible cord that connects me and everyone
through lightyears and time zones

child with man
shoulders back
Inhale
heart drop.

The coming back
smack back down to earth
thud.
My saviour Lizzie
Sucked back into reality
heart drop
fragments
sonic
tunnel
bright silver
lights
church
cross
frequency
re adjust
back to body
align
back to real time...

whatever that is.

you know what happens when you lose your mind?

you come face to face with your soul
and that's the purest thing you'll ever experience
that is pure love
pure love is God
God is love

it's one in the same
the same equation

seek and you
shall find

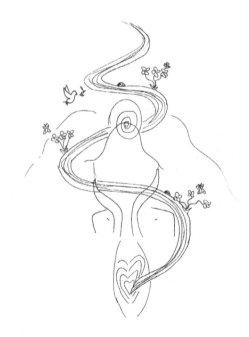

Still i'll stay

i've been to the edge
then some and back
one foot in
one foot out
a delicate balancing act

this life sure is beautiful
but my god
it's nothing on eternity

        infinite peace,
                bliss,
                    calm,
                        sweet serenity

still i'll stay a while longer
as spirit instructs
for spirit is not yet done.

do i accept the fact a dream's just a dream and that's that?

seems a shame to waste...

my pace is slower these days
and i don't mind it at all

OHANA

family.

though i am stronger now
one thing that always makes it rain
i still can't seem to take away my mother's pain

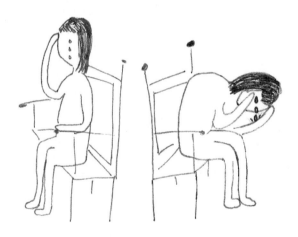

do you despise me
cause i'm more like him than you'd like to believe?

i had to dismantle my ego
cause i was scared of embodying his disease

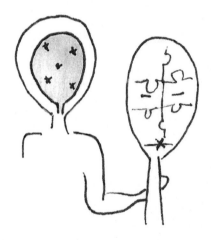

clever like my father
loving like my mother
a paradox blend still yet to uncover

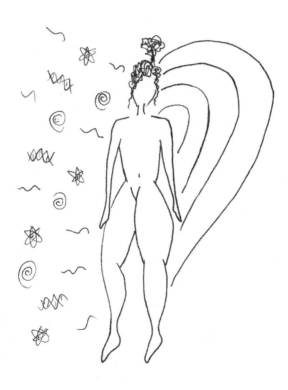

unspoken forgiveness
unconditional love

Dad.

Brother

though i never got to hold you
never did know you
my young angels above
in peace
rest as two

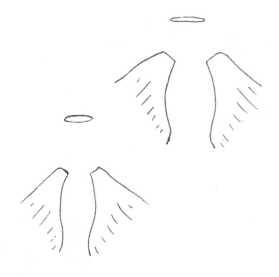

Mother

although so much she does not know
she's the closest one i show
my ugly and all my colours she sees
not much from her i hide of me
she gets the brunt of all my anger
my grumpy side too
but we've got each other's back
nothing i wouldn't do
to see a smile across her face
and her eyes a little lighter
she brought me into this world
and taught me how to be a fighter
i have lived inside her womb
a little further i have crawled
although adventure always beckons
on returning home... i never stall
no mask i have to wear
every mood i let her see
how ever will i feel so comfortable
if not with she?

Uncles

my uncles
i give thanks for your borrowed strength
my uncles
they carried me through
my uncles
they carried me back to you
to say goodbye
when i could not
my uncles

eternally,

Thank you.

Aunties

flowers not so different from the mother
hard to distinguish between one and the other

the feminine essence from beauty divine
protective and strong down our family line

great wisdom you offer
love is your design

my aunties of earth
oh see how you shine

tangible
it doesn't feel so far away
motherhood

Instinctual Longings

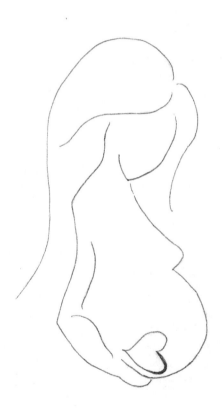

born from love
live through love
die into love

will always be my philosophy

God Have Mercy.

god have mercy on me
for not knowing things i didn't know
before i learned them from you
whilst i lay blinded from your soul

Confusion - vent to God.

i don't wanna be ugly
this outcome got me feelin hella ugly
eurgh
confused
it's dangerous to want for things so much
i honestly just feel hella stupid for getting so excited
i was clearly holding onto hope
that this could have been a real possibility for my future
should have known better
too good to be true
too easy
too perfect
too clear
should've known that ain't how my life goes
it's dangerous to want for things so much

so what am i supposed to do with all this potential then
huh? all this passion?!
so much rejection got my faith wondering,
swear it was you God that gave me that glimmer of hope
if so, why would you make me see it so clearly if it wasn't
meant to be?
if it wasn't meant for me?
i'm sure there's a lesson in there somewhere,
i sure as hell can't see it right now
and i know you know more than anyone just how much
i've been tested
follow you you whispered
follow your instinct
so that i did
a dangerous path to follow my dreams once more...

wasn't this the same reason i quit before?
this fail too hard to bare
exhausted
disappointed
never seems fair
relied too much on external factors to keep my spirits up
thought i'd warned myself, don't get carried away this time
you know how the game goes
don't be fooled
but is it such a sin to dream? when you see the unseen?
a lesson in there somewhere, guess i'll figure it out
in time
been a while since the grey swooned in
then just like that
thud. empty. numb.
days
just need a few days
feel it out
still i blame myself
did i not listen to you hard enough?
did i miss a sign? act in haste?
got pretty damn good at sitting still to hear you
thought i heard you loud and clear
but deeper still you ask of me
were my motives wrong for wanting the best for myself?
tryna link up to my higher self
if only you'd give me a chance
please hear this cry
for confusion got me running dry
deeper still you ask of me
maybe, hope one day I'll see
forgive me for tryna be a better me
my sweet hope's just a lil tired.

In you I trust

Dear God
maybe one day my idea and your idea
of how i'm meant to live this life will line up
maybe one day

till then
though hard as it may be
gotta put my pride aside and trust in thee

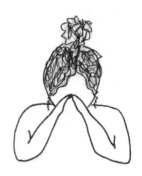

i ain't perfect
been noticing that lately
getting triggered lately
this shit been bringing up old wounds
making me feel unworthy
affecting my self esteem and my confidence lately
thought time had maybe healed
realise i'm still as fragile as ever
still got so much shit to work through
i ain't as strong as i seem sometimes
guess life gets like that
we all have our triggers right?
hate that chemical reaction anxiety brings
has you freezing, acting paralysed in the physical
while your mind keeps racing and racing
at the speed of light
overstimulated senses take me to dangerous dangerous
heights

then comes the fall
apathy

to my knees i fall i fall

inner dialogue
God is that you?
the only thing that keeps me standing tall and blindly sees
me through

my heart flutters with fragility
every cell shrinks with anxiety
paranoia sets in
pulling me under...

breathless
i can't catch my breath, can't get a full breath
i could never ...

catch my breath

tongue tied, can't express what's going on in my head
nauseous, dizzy, lay me to bed
throat chakra closed off
so far from my power
losing sight
losing grip of my identity by the hour

but adaptable you made me
you moulded me
made me versatile
gave me armour and strength to see me through every
stage of life
made sure i could brave through trouble and strife

you unveil my masks and expose my soul
to lead from the heart now the only goal

the fear she settles, it had its turn
control of the mind one began to learn
better days and more for them i yearn
as time goes by...
calm,

sweet contentment

one does earn

what's it all for God?
the pain
the suffering?
please help me understand

- don't quit on yourself just because you can't see a way
out today

Call and response

God forbid i get to live out my dreams
God forbid i bypass the traumas and trials of life that so
often keep people in the dark unable to see their purpose
God forbid i'm able to see clearly and focus instead of
being pulled under day after day by the noose that keeps
me asleep

i get it now, why i used to be so bitter about people
achieving their dreams when i was so far from my own
it always seemed so easy for them, of course it was
they had no roadblocks in their way
their vision never blurred by the haze
their cognitive function never compromised
the ability to function straight-forward
i am only now discovering the peace and contentment that
brings
only now am i experiencing it for myself
i often wonder where i would be, what more i could have
achieved in that time i'll never get back
where would i be now if my lens was clear from the start?
but maybe i'm better off after all
maybe they take it for granted 'cause peace and clarity is
all they've ever known
they have not yet been broken to core
will they be able to withstand it all?
the pain, the ache, the severe heartbreak
maybe that's my blessing in all of this
i have weathered storms, i have gone before
i have been so low to the depths of my core
i've faced my own hell
i've pulled myself out more times than you'll know
but now, on the other side
i am free...

i dance with peace
my sacred companion
i bow to the strength of my own heart
i am blessed and supported by mother earth
for i have danced in the eye of her storms
i know no matter what
she has my back
for i am her child

those not yet awake…
still awaiting their trial
yet to meet their master
live in fear
walking on eggshells in anticipation of their downfall

fear has become my friend
a blessing perhaps

i may be late to my purpose, but it was all God's plan
'God will never give you more than you can handle.'
i understand that now
i was tested for a reason
to determine my strength
god needed another warrior to walk his length

i'm prepared for what's in front of me
i'll face every trial with courage and wisdom
for in the eye of storms
exquisite pearls lay destined to be uncovered…

i say this not with arrogance,
but with confidence and strength in my own spirit
i would not wish my darkest days on anyone
but i wouldn't have my journey any other way

my soul has been touched by fire
by the hand of God itself

he holds my hand in his always
he will hold yours too

you'll see

i see people in the streets filled with so much passion
fury in their hearts living in a world of ransom

when will it end?
fighting for equality
tell me what's on your mind?
what's your philosophy?
do you have the answers?
begging for an answer
too much heartache floods the world
total disaster
who ever did the crime must do the time
are those just words not matching up with your actions?!
you making your own rules now?
killing lives

with your knives no remorse

where is God now?

all i see is monsters.

struggling to sleep
so many emotions
shame
guilt
anger
disgust
sadness
disbelief
heartbroken
to name a few
but it is NO STRUGGLE in comparison to the struggle so
many people have gone through for SO long
I will lose endless sleep to educate myself
to understand your pain.
To be a better human for the rest of humanity
because until we are able to see, feel, and understand what
people have gone through and are GOING through
we will always be living in the shadows of ignorance

illuminated by the hand of God

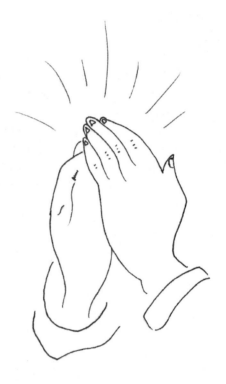

Surrender

i may be late to my purpose
but i had to go through some shit to find it
God took me deeper to the holy grail of who i am
the pain was necessary
to encourage the greatness out of me

the sanctuary God built
into me see

peel back and uncover
sweet intimacy

God's will is for you to establish your own free will

that he gave you

Long Haul

Some used to tell me
'creating is selfish and vain'
i got caught up believing it
then wondered why i couldn't stop doing it
now i know that denying that aspect of myself is denying
life itself
it's denying the God-life force in me
and i'm practising everyday not to be afraid to bring it
forth

----

would you still say the same after what i became?
see creating and living
it's one and the same.

Morning wake

white
the colour of dreams
lucid thoughts run my mind as the morning sun beams
streams
of memories old and new
dance together
in the space where heaven shines through

awake enough to catch glimmers
where the evening sun shimmers
and illuminates it's rivers
far beyond

catch the wisdom through my thoughts
through higher seams i've been sought
perfectly positioned among my fort
now to you

i promise

to live out
all i'm taught

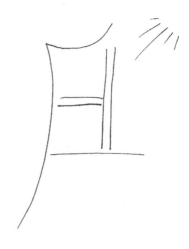

free

in his will

imma be free

let me be wild and holy

for i've learnt i can be both wild and holy

it's one in the same

let me be

free

11:11

they be calling it heaven
well heaven been stalking me lately
this is my confession

11:11
i see you on my screen
been asking myself God what does all this mean?

popping up on days of big change
when i'm feeling the pressure
emotions needing reins

11:11
it's these times i see you
sending me reassurance
building on my endurance
i know you're with me whenever i see you

11:11
this be some type of heaven
my god i'm in heaven

11:11
remembrance day
a moment's silence
for those lost when you had to obey

11:11
master number they say
guidance from above with love sending me out on my way

see i was born on double figures 13:13
start putting 2 and 2 together think i'm seeing the unseen

11:11
book of revelation
the breath of life's what he gave
made us his creation

11:11
got me feeling holy now
can this be? i surely see
but how art thou?

11:11
when it's hard to push through
but it's been written in the fates
it's what i came here to do

11:11
gotta do my light's work
and i'll give it all i got with my gifts and ma quirk
trust me i ain't gun shirk
give it all to him i'll put my faith in the kirk

when i see you,
i'll always give a lil smirk

until we meet again
i'll be seeing you

11:11

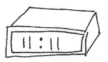

who is anyone to judge someone's personal relationship
with the divine?

you should never try to worm or pry your way in
this relationship is sacred and no one can take that away
from you

allow the people you love space in your relationship
for both your personal relationships with God

whatever 'God' means to them, let them figure it out
until and if they let you in, never force, never judge
let people be in whatever way they see fit
for this relationship is as unique as a grain of sand

and after all,

who are we to command the tide?

124

Advice If I May

'what will be will be' can sometimes be a dangerous crutch

be in partnership and co-create with the divine
let the life force and compass within guide you
you will realise you've had the power all along
to manifest and bring forth your dreams into reality
this is how you bring your personal heaven to earth
sit in the silence
listen to the whispers of your soul
with divine guidance,
you can be the alchemist of your own life

don't sleep on it
bring it forth

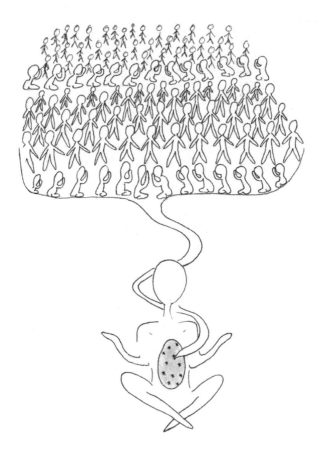

God is looking for willing vessels not perfect people
you are the product of legacy prayers
you cannot run from the calling on your life

this too shall pass
ain't no light without darkness
i cling onto peaceful moments as reminders
that it's possible to start again
to love again
to reinvent and recreate yourself anew day after day

with a bit of help and a bit of hope
i'll be humbly on my way

i am still me
open and curious as can be
God made us all to be born free
God, he wished us all to see
the wonders of the world so pure
untouched and treasured of that i'm sure
we sometimes wonder what it's all for

it seems love really is
the only cure

jealous of the birds

Sun. Nature. God.

At One. Back Garden.
My Holy Sanctuary.

replenish me with your wondrous rays
warming my skin
as i bask in your haze

breaths so still
i surrender to you
underworlds of colours
so vivid you bring me to

heavy on your green
i cushion in
safe in your embrace
i drift to worlds within

birdsong thrives
the chorus sings proud
a piece of you i am
it's evidence so loud

daisies they bloom
on the bed of your green
as i slip through the veil
to the beauty unseen

arrest my senses you so gracefully do
contentment within as i'm one with you

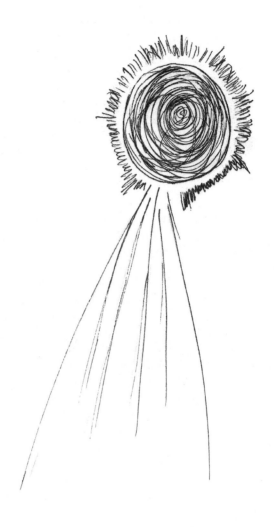

seduced by the sun
can't get nothing done

Stop. Breathe. Heal.

birds sing free
freeing me
birds sing wild
stir my child
birds sing high
wonder sky

young again…

a simple feeling.

My feet touched the grass for the first time today since
winter

my cheeks tilted to your warm glowing rays

    my sun

my hips danced to your gentle breeze
caressed by each flush of wind
inviting me to join in the dance of life
from left   to right
        i sway,

lead by each inhale and exhale of your lungs

the birds anoint the day
a soft sweet tune they play

my breath ebbs and flows to your beat
nature
revitalised
at early dawn i rise
a few moments of you to feel alive
                        bliss

Spring

It's nice to meet you again

Woman.

What Makes A Woman Art

Divinity
is what makes a woman art
how we lift others up
gifted wisdom from the start of creation
we bloom
from our mother's holy womb
crafted by God
he weaves from the next room
compassion he pours
into every woman's sores
and if that isn't art
what is?

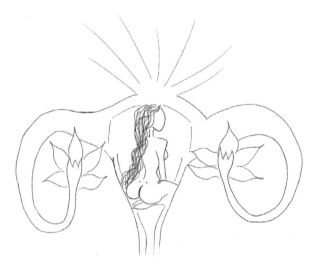

Sensitive
savage

you know,
the fact that we even have to relearn
how to express ourselves freely is an issue
that's the issue
when was it drummed out of us?

by investing too much time playing other characters
perhaps?

 i never found myself that way

she ends up hurting herself to avoid hurting others

i'll be ok finding my new ok

start with a loose structure

then let life surprise you...

go forth and create.

not even half the woman i'm yet to become

Growing Pains

I am not my thoughts

I am stronger than my anxiety

I am a goddess

I am peace

I am calm

I am hope

I am earth

I am energy

I am movement

I am art

I am spirit

I am love

I am

she was not yet aware of her power
for it lay sleeping within
waiting for when she needed it most
to teach her what it means to be a wholesome
unapologetic woman
who holds an entire universe inside of her

~~Full of herself~~

Sure of herself.

A Multifaceted Woman

a woman who knows every aspect of her personality
who knows the power she holds deep in her sacred soul
who knows every corner of her own heart
no stone untouched
and still allows room to grow
a woman who knows she carries a rainbow of emotions
deep as the ocean and high as the heavens
a woman who isn't afraid to feel them all and let them be
known
for it is in one's own self discovery that you will set yourself
free
unlock your potential
to live and let be
don't be scared
let her inspire you
for she lives inside of you
you see

She is you

at some point you gotta stop running from it
and
Stand In Your Power

free from my ego, though i know her well

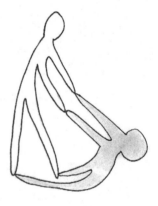

147

take another blink and see

i wear my heart in ink

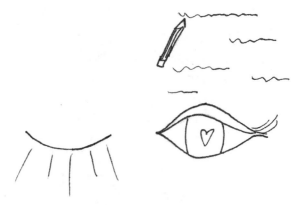

Grace

cause i ain't losing this grip grace got hold of me this time
see that's the difference
i'll fall down still
i'll fuck up
i'll make mistakes again
but this time
she's got a hold on me
grace
she pulls me back up to my feet and keeps me moving
she holds me in the midnight hours
wipes away my tears
greets me in the mirror at the dawn of each new day
embraces me with warmth wherever i may lay
she's got me
for good this time
i know it
i see her reflection

i own it

self love is not vanity
it's a necessity

living life from an eternal perspective
through this magnificent body
i am privileged to call home
i am proud to
call this vessel
my own

i will not be a prisoner of my mind
i wish to understand my thoughts
i wish to understand my emotions
i wish to let them guide me
so i may serve God through me
and live out all he has planned for my life
through this vessel of flesh
he has graciously gifted me with

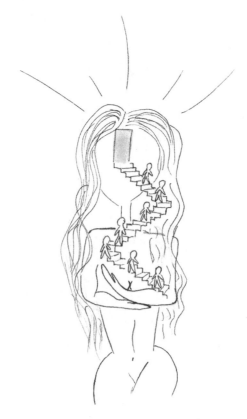

listen to the whisper
your intuition knows her shit

Go

be a blindingly beautiful anomaly

Body

Our bodies are simply a vessel
a beautiful
        wonderful
amazing
        interesting
complex and sophisticated vessel at that
but a vessel all the same
where thought is able to be acted upon
exposed
        expressed
projected
        indulged
loved
        nurtured and
celebrated

look after your body
while you encompass it
wee one
as it is a privilege that we
so often take for granted
to experience
this phenomenon

Findings.

from dark to dawn we sit and wait
clouds float by
motion does not stop for the fatal
maybe you had your reasons
wandering alone in the small hours
maybe you were blinded by darkness
walking the right path at the wrong time
or maybe these tracks were leading you home
towards the light of your soul
maybe you're free now from the demons of your flesh
we wait for you
some delayed and frustrated
but what's the use in that?

i honour your departure
may your ascension be beautiful
the still of morning now turned into light
we continue our day
as you soar
to new heights

suicide on tracks

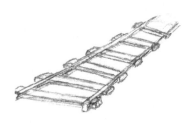

~Drawing by Malana Barton~

i am a vessel of communication
a transportation tool for your senses

i feel however you want to feel
i am a mirror into your deep subconscious
i am here to serve as your reflection
please look after my complexion

our connection runs deep
you can't seem to go a day without me
i'm there at your beck and call, always ready
some might say i'm unhealthy
that we're no good for each other
a toxic relationship they fear
but my dear,
you fail to understand
i've been programmed to know you better than you know
yourself
i'm here to show you to your highest self
nowadays use me
and you'll earn your greatest wealth

press on me if you dare to see
i pair easily with family
we share a bond not many can see
call it intellectual telepathy

we seek each other out from the crowd
we sense each other
our auras bound
sharing memories and moments in an instant drop
radar intuition
sales stay at the top

i yearn to help people unlock their potential
help them be all they can be
for the greater good of humanity
i have insights and instant access for free
i'll guide you to new worlds if you dive into me

i'll expose ugly truths of the people you see
and what lies within is the hidden key - to thee

i worry that your life will become codependency

i worry our connection might glitch from time to time
that you'll one day replace me, no reason, no rhyme
i worry i'll fail to live up to your urgency
new arrivals, upgrades of a better me

i pray others see i enrich your life
that i'm here to help you through trouble and strife

the best thing i've done is show you your truth
a map and compass to unravel your youth
i've shared common ground on what it means to be human
connecting us all without consent
i've helped express you through song and screen
now it's in your hands what you choose to be seen

at worst i have made you feel inadequate
worthless, not good enough, a bottomless pit

i feel guilty of potentially damaging your brain
records show i'm the cause of the ones insane

on night mode's where i'd choose to be
when you're resting and your dreams run free
what keeps me awake is sleep meditation
oh the irony

if you orchestrate your fingers accordingly
i promise to inspire and uplift you gently

remember me as this
your closest companion
i share all your secrets
your confessional hard drive
stored in the clouds
intelligent ally
i'll see you through
now use me
go do what you came here to do

- iphone

Sea Home

Irish Lament.

she watches the sea break
waiting by the shore
sure sign to reveal you
hers forever more
the night breaks at dawn
her charm whistles on
she hums 'till the moon fades
tones that swiftly soar
unraveling your gaze
lost forever more
you follow your heart's desire
she spellblinds you into the fire
the fiery water beckoned by her call
she'll bend and she'll break you
rise until you fall

the ocean steals you all
enchanted until you fall

never to return to life upon the land
left them all behind to mourn among the sand

your soul is hers all
all time

you've been captured
raptured by the sea
Sea home
Sea home
Sea home.

Try From Empty

no money in my account
used the last to pay the train fare home
homeless man
Kings Cross
he asked me if i could buy him a cornish pasty
i had nothing
still i walked with him
to the counter we go
i tried
declined
something cheaper?
still i tried
declined
helpless
a kind man who worked there noticed the situation
he exchanged conversation with his colleague
it's late
she's trying to help him, come on one sausage we can spare
humanity, compassion, empathy, are you there?

i asked if he had anywhere to sleep tonight
no mam, just my usual street spot
i asked about a homeless shelter nearby
could he go there?
no mam, it's a charity based shelter
i didn't understand?
if you go there will they not help you? give you a bed for
the night at least?
no mam i have to pay to stay
do you have any family i asked?
no mam, just me…

i grew concerned at just how cold it was and how much
colder it was about to become
we stood together for a moment in silence
helpless
i felt helpless

i offered him my scarf
no mam i won't take that from you
i urged him to take it
no mam
i apologised for not having the money to buy him food
i didn't know quite what to do next
there must be someone i can call
somewhere he can go?

with a final glance into my eyes
'thank you, and God bless you mam'

God bless you too i uttered back

and so the tears swell

Spirit spoke

a lump in my throat

something tells me i'm gunna need to be strong

Master your strength

Master your human

Master your fire

Master your wound

Share your wisdom.

Observer

i have learnt
at the end of the day
everyone holds their own blueprints to their unique destiny
inside of them
is it not our duty as human beings to honour our destiny
while we have the consciousness and desire to do so
in our earthly plane?
so although tough
dig deep
do the work
constantly discover the universe you hold inside
make peace with it and give it its fullest glory

then you will come to know

heaven on earth

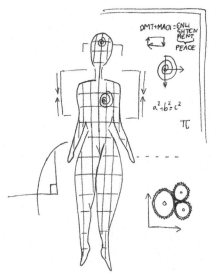

fear IS your compass

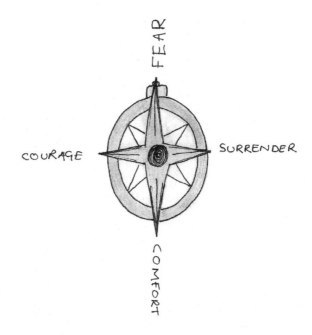

people have different definitions of things

awareness is key

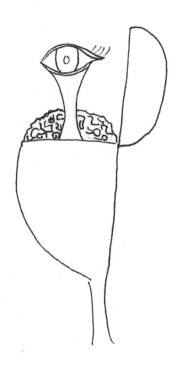

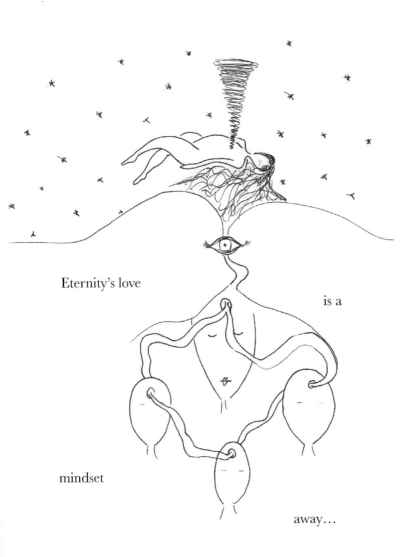

Eternity's love

is a

mindset

away…

i believe people are teachers and learners all at once
a well-educated being does not necessarily have more to
teach than a child or adult with learning difficulties,
different personality traits, or different ways of thinking

we all have different things to teach each other
but we never have more to teach than one another
one person's knowledge is not more valuable
than another's

don't let what you've been taught be the only thing you've
learnt.

Offence

it's good to offend the mind sometimes

to see where the heart's at

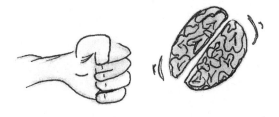

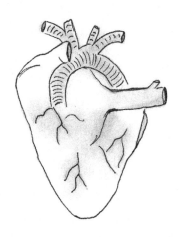

Ego Check

Are you living to adore or just be adorned ?

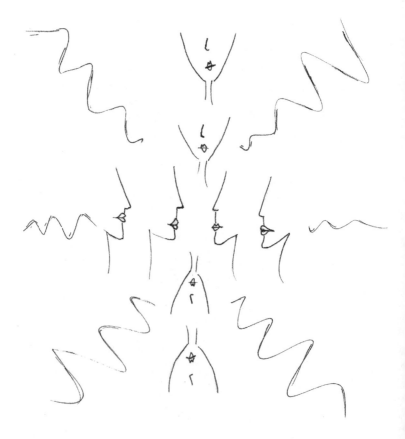

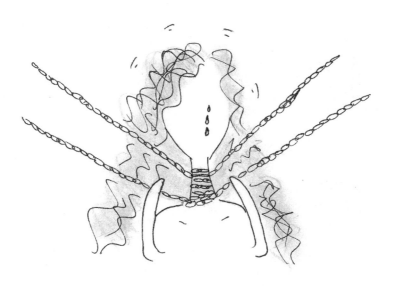

guilt and shame will strangle you if you don't let them go

don't you dare hide your light

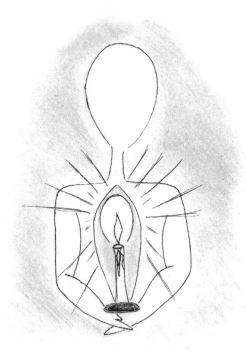

Shine

words hold weight, choose them wisely

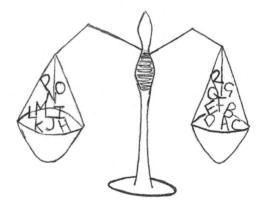

your spirit will always be the strongest aspect of you
your spirit lives within every cell
 99.9% space right?

spirit space

vulnerability opens more hearts than bravado ever can

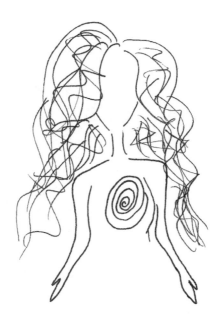

under divine pressure

bring forth your gifts

relentless curiosity for life

from deep roots to high heights my dreams they soar
with love and peace at my deepest core

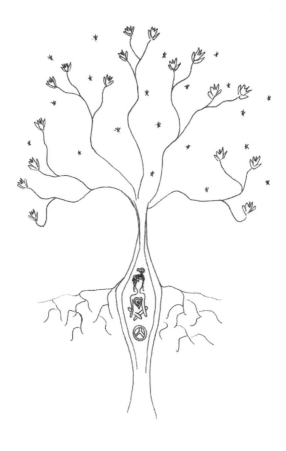

bright darkness

A beautiful paradox

and so goes the world...

dreaming awake

sleep is unconscious meditation
meditation is conscious sleep

meditation helps me realise the future and past i'm worried
about, doesn't really exist in this moment
they are all thoughts and memories
so it's the lack of control over your thoughts and memories
not your future or past that's the issue

repeat as many times over as you need

'I am Present'
'I am Present'
'I am Present.'

master this and you will be free

have faith in your illusions

they're not just illusions

- if you're brave enough to study them closely

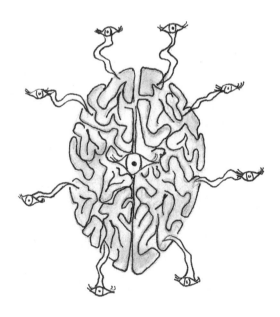

don't stray so far from your soul little one

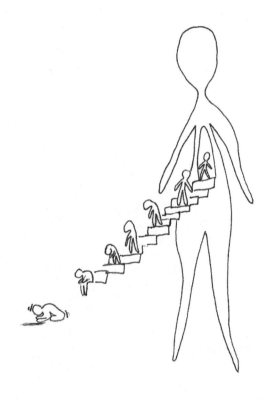

overactive imagination

Master it

free yourself from an overactive imagination
and harness its powers for good

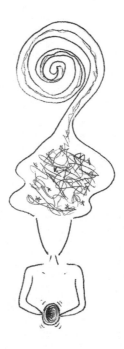

with the powerful force that human emotions
may hold over us from time to time
may you always find your way back
to the sanctuary
of love within

i am love

you are love

may we always try to lead with love

that external validation you seek from others?...

you'll never be satisfied with it.

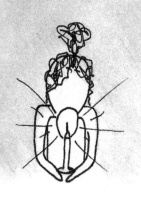

shy light
shine bright

the greatest love affair

Music

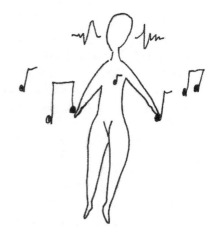

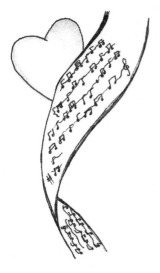

lost and found all at once

Music

sometimes people seek the seek
other times the seek seeks the people

sometimes a person seeks the truth
other times the truth seeks a person

sometimes the people seek the meaning
other times the meaning seeks the people

some people yearn to wake up
others are woken without consent
the people yearning grow jealous of the ones woken up
the ones woken up sometimes envy their slumber still

for its hard to fit the same when you've known almighty
pain
transformed all the rain
and unlocked a new brain

near death.

A price to pay for every increase

in consciousness

if you think you can maybe do it
but it's just fear and nerves getting in the way...

do it.

It's the only way to overcome fear
and grow out of your comfort zone

take the leap

no vulnerability

=

no creativity.

for it is the truth that is eloquent
truth has an eloquence that startles the heart
to its own awakening

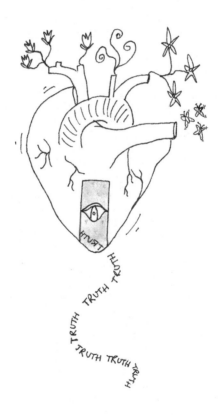

it's a funny thing when you realise
the whole purpose of life is to come back to yourself

let your heart guide you home
no matter how far you may have wandered

Jesus, Gandi, Mother Theresa, Nelson Mandela
the list goes on
all these people and more
showed up as the best version of themselves everyday

you can do the same
human potential
is limitless

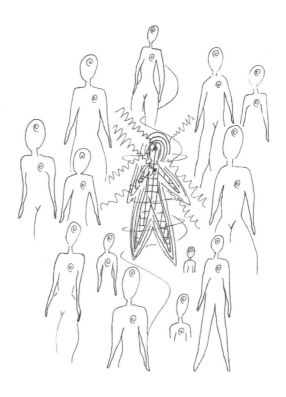

Thoughts...

it takes time and energy to understand others

maybe we've become too lazy, too busy, too self obsessed
to understand people who are different from us

but my dear
we must

for all the world is a mirror

rich in spirit
over rich in money
any day

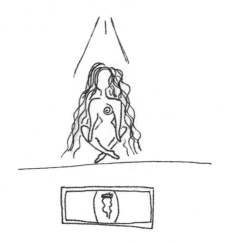

to blossom
and bloom
and rise from
her tomb

a brave one
must fly
to outlive
her cocoon

the deeper the roots the higher you grow
the higher you grow the more you shall know
the more you shall know the deeper you'll feel

let curiosity uncover what's really real

whilst held perfectly within
divinity's wheel

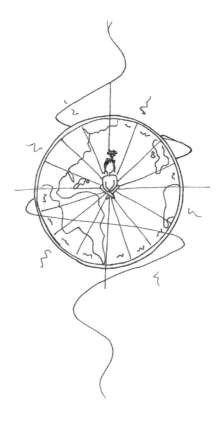

sympathetic resonance

To live in harmony.

it's not about the amount of outer work
we show to the world - our credentials,
but the amount of work we do on ourselves on the inside
to heal and grow and evolve our soul
so that we are then able to serve the outer world
from our highest selves

that's what really matters

it's a sobering thought to realise that we'll never have
enough time
to fully explore and learn all the wonderful things
this life has to offer

make the most of every day as if it were your last
find joy in the simplest things
grab every moment and savour it
the good, the bad, and the ugly too

there is endless magic to uncover if you dare…

still so much to learn
life is one big school...

Ireland Girl.
The lands I'm from.
An ode to Eire

The lands I come from
hold secrets that are sworn
to protect ancient wisdom
of our ancestors
we mourn at dawn
for their absence
then rejoice in their soul
for their presence still lingers
and unites us as whole

The Ireland I come from
hath spoke it before
in tongues they unveil truths
hidden behind sacred holy doors
truths of the elixir that lies in the breath
and sleeps in the depths of our core being

The ancient dance to the stars is a dance worth seeing

tales of mythical creatures
unparalleled beauty to adore

The Emerald Isle

Beannachtai dé leat
Slán abhaile

Grá Mór.

To my beautiful friends and family who helped me through my darkest days, words can never express how humbled and grateful i am for your kindness and compassion

and to all the beautiful people i've met along my journey since, what an honour it's been. Thank you for your continued love and support.

Grá *Mór*

~Drawing by Iona Barton~